Affiliate Marketing

(A systematic approach towards the creation of passive income, attainment of financial independence, and achievement of success in online marketing

(The Latest and Enhanced Approaches for Generating Online Revenue through Digital Marketing)

Steven Meunier

TABLE OF CONTENT

Your Complimentary Supplementary Material

In this section, we shall delve into the topic of developing supplementary content to cater to your target audience. You shall provide this content complimentary when customers acquire your affiliate offers. It is commonly known as the practice of Offer Stacking.

Merely obtaining individuals to register for an affiliate offer does not preclude extending them additional incentives should they make a purchase via your provided link. This is a widely prevalent practice. In addition, it contributes to our overarching objective of providing assistance to individuals. We are desirous of extending an additional value proposition to individuals.

They are making a purchase of our affiliate offer, nevertheless, it does not indicate that their issue has been entirely resolved. It does not imply that the company with whom we have an affiliation has thoroughly considered what would be beneficial for their customers.

Additionally, while it is possible that the affiliate offer provides solutions to a portion of their issue, it is necessary to incorporate supplementary elements tailored to your particular target audience for the affiliate offer to be truly relevant and effective. Alternatively, it may be necessary to incorporate this additional value in order to establish a competitive edge among other affiliates in the industry. We are unable to all engage in the sale of identical products. To differentiate your offer effectively, it is imperative to develop a distinct value proposition.

Therefore, there are numerous justifications for incorporating your own supplementary materials and augmenting your offering. It will effectively motivate individuals to make purchases through your link, as opposed to other alternatives, thus positioning you as a knowledgeable and supportive expert by offering additional value without any supplementary cost.

An illustration of this scenario would be offering a complimentary supplementary training program for users who want to embark on the utilization of the software. Rather than immersing oneself recklessly in software with potentially limited documentation, especially considering the lack of established help articles in many early-stage startup software due to their focus on development, one can familiarize themselves with the software by exploring its functionalities. By gaining firsthand knowledge of its workings, one can then embark on the creation of a supplementary training course to facilitate effective learning for users, ensuring they derive maximum value from their monetary investment.

This would be particularly advantageous for your business, especially considering that each signup would result in a recurring commission for your benefit. It proves advantageous when your purchasers possess adequate proficiency in utilizing the software. Alternatively, if this situation persists, their comprehension may be compromised, leading to a potential decline in the recurring revenue generated on a monthly basis. However, by investing sufficient effort into creating a concise instructional program that demonstrates the proper utilization of the software, individuals are more likely to retain it for an extended period of time, thereby leading to increased financial gain.

You have the ability to donate or distribute items such as:

- Short program

- Digital book

- Printed publication in physical form

- Mentoring or advising • Guidance or assistance • Collaboration or support

- Inspection sheets • Assessment forms • Verification lists • Inventory records • Audit documents

- Audio-visual presentations

- Online seminars • Virtual presentations • Web-based lectures

- Associations

- Pre-designed formats

- Expertly crafted manuals

- Exercise materials or supplementary study resources

- Comprehensive service provided on your behalf

These tools can be utilized to pre-frame individuals, assisting in establishing a connection between your affiliate offer and their specific circumstances, thereby elucidating the importance of your product/service to them.

For instance, when considering the sale of ClickFunnels, a funnel building program, to dentists, it is possible that they may lack proficiency in its utilization or fail to grasp the benefits it holds for their practice.

One can introduce the concept of sales funnels to individuals by presenting blog articles that outline the rationale behind their necessity. This can be followed by directing them to a bridge page specifically designed to educate them about ClickFunnels. Ultimately, upon their registration, an e-book or training course may be made available to them. The offer stack has the capability to demonstrate to them the precise manner in which they can effectively utilize the software tailored to their specific business category. You also have the option to offer complimentary, readily available templates. Now they have established comprehensive guidelines detailing the construction of a dental-focused funnel, ultimately aiding in their expansion, acquisition of a broader client base, and augmentation of revenue streams. Increased revenue for their business results in additional monthly payments to ClickFunnels, thereby ensuring a more stable and secure monthly income for your business.

These bonuses should be provided to individuals who make purchases through your affiliate links at no cost. I kindly request that no additional charges be applied despite the effort invested in this matter. It aligns with the same line of thought that aims to provide customers with enhanced value in exchange for their money, thereby distinguishing oneself from other sellers.

Please retrieve a sheet of paper and carefully consider your audience, contemplate your affiliate offer, and deliberate on any supplementary information which may prove valuable to them, but is not encompassed within the aforementioned offer.

A different illustration of this phenomenon can be observed through the implementation I enacted for the Funnelytics affiliate program. Over the course of time, I have developed various funnel templates for individuals. Instead of attempting to devise their own funnels, I offer them fundamental funnel maps from which they can derive and strategize their own funnels.

Even without a Pro account, these templates can be accessed and utilized at no cost. The Funnelytics account is offered without charge, and users can make full use of its capabilities. It is an exceptionally desirable incentive that has garnered positive reception, with individuals willingly providing their email addresses in exchange. Not only was I successfully acquiring individuals' interest in Funnelytics and associating them with my affiliate offer, but I also obtained their email addresses.

I highly recommend that you consider registering for the free-level account of Funnelytics in the near future as we outline and strategize our affiliate funnel. The affiliate program has ceased to operate, however, it remains a useful software that I am inclined to suggest to individuals.

Acquiring leads is a crucial component of this entire procedure. It is not advisable to directly redirect individuals to your affiliate offer, as such action eliminates any sense of connection, rapport, and the opportunity for future contact. Consequently, you would not be able to address any additional concerns they may have or supply them with affiliate links to further beneficial products.

This is an additional advantage of having an offer stack. You have the capability to avail yourself of the opportunity whereby individuals sign up for your offers and subsequently enroll in the affiliate offers as well. Several affiliate companies do not provide the email addresses of individuals who register.

Consequently, it is necessary to establish a means of gathering this information beforehand, prior to directing individuals through the designated channels.

Utilizing email marketing platforms enables the incorporation of a redirect feature post-form submission. Individuals have the option to input their personal information such as their name and email address into the provided form in order to receive the additional incentives that you offer. The email of the individual is enlisted in your records, enabling you to subsequently include them in your email automation processes. The aforementioned email sequence should subsequently furnish them with additional complimentary items and meaningful content, or alternatively, present to them the subsequent product that you aspire to deliver. Perhaps it could be a creation of your own, especially if you have dedicated significant efforts to developing your business to the extent you've mentioned.

That is the inherent elegance of the situation. You have the opportunity to obtain their email address, enabling them to be included in your automated email sequence and added to your mailing list. Consequently, you can seamlessly guide them towards the affiliate offer through an automated redirection process.

Considering their recent enrollment for the bonuses, there is a greater probability that they will proceed to enroll for the affiliate offer. Subsequently, you will effortlessly redirect them to your affiliate offer, while strategically preserving a valuable point of contact for potential future interactions, as opposed to directly directing them to the affiliate offer without procuring their email address.

This represents a significant milestone in the establishment of your automated systems, which will aid in the attainment of the level of personal freedom you ardently desire. Gather contact information, incorporate individuals into automated email distribution lists, and configure the delivery of all offer stack deliverables through electronic mail. Nurture and foster connections with individuals on automatic pilot. Sell on autopilot. Generate passive income while you are at rest.

The practice of stacking offers possesses considerable inherent value, as evident from the aforementioned observations. It is an immensely potent instrument that is virtually indispensable for the establishment of your email roster and the growth of your affiliate enterprise.

14

Affiliate Marketing Introduction

Engaging in the subsidiary advertising industry has become significantly more manageable due to the extensive availability and accessibility of the Internet. Its current state of affairs is significantly more straightforward in comparison to the era when individuals had to rely on telephones and other means of information transmission solely to access real-time updates on the progress of their program.

Given the accessibility of innovation and assuming that the individual is engaging in telecommuting, a typical day in their routine would resemble the following...

Upon awakening and following the consumption of a meal, the computer is employed to examine recent advancements within the company. After careful consideration, it is apparent that there may be new elements to update and protocols to adhere to.

The site configuration necessitates updating. The advertiser acknowledges that a well-designed website has the potential to enhance the acquisition of individuals from the visiting audience. It can also facilitate the offspring's conversion rates.

With that task completed, it is now opportune to introduce the affiliate program to directories that outline associate programs. These registries serve as a mechanism to attract individuals to enrol in your affiliate program. A concrete strategy for enhancing the member program!

It is imperative to accurately and judiciously ascertain the profits derived from your subsidiaries at this juncture. There exist telephonic inquiries and dispatches to locate. Please verify whether those individuals are prospective clients who are examining the products. Recording the contact information for future reference, as it appears to be a viable source moving forward.

There are numerous resources to organize. Promotional materials, banners, button advertisements, and product recommendations are distributed as the advertiser recognizes the effectiveness of these strategies in augmenting sales. It is advisable to maintain a noticeable presence and accessibility.

The subsidiary advertiser has noted that there are inquiries from the guests that require attention. It is imperative that this be completed expeditiously. An unanswered email can have a detrimental impact on client satisfaction. In order to establish the effectiveness and efficiency of the offshoot, a more concerted effort ought to be made to prioritize and concentrate on specific requests. Everyone should be treated with fairness and clients, irrespective of their disposition, are typically not the most reserved. Prompt and effective response that is expected to demonstrate proficiency while maintaining a friendly demeanor.

While engaged in fulfilling all the necessary tasks, the marketer actively engages in a discourse platform where they interact with fellow affiliates and participants of the same program. This facilitates the discussion of strategies for effectively promoting their products.

There are matters to be acquired knowledge of, and this process is perpetual. Offering suggestions and counsel is a respectable means of demonstrating assistance. There could conceivably be others who would wish to join and could find themselves enthralled by the ongoing discourse. There is no harm in anticipating the opportunities that lie ahead.

The brochures and electronic magazines were recently updated in advance, therefore it is now opportune for the affiliate marketer to assess any emerging developments in the industry. This will be further elaborated upon in the advertiser's publication to be disseminated to both existing and prospective customers.

These equivalent distributions serve as a valuable tool in ensuring one is well-informed about the latest products that have been introduced. The advertiser has established a proposition and promotion that customers may wish to be cognizant of. Furthermore, it is imperative for them to remain cognizant of the designated deadline for these offers as delineated in the disseminations.

This opportunity allows for the expression of gratitude towards the individuals who have provided valuable assistance to the advertiser in facilitating progress and pursuing expansion. In stark contrast to citing individuals, their locations, and the actions they have undertaken to ensure successful outcomes.
It is evident that this information will be disseminated through the bulletins.

Among the more notable data that has been compiled thus far.

The advertiser possesses the capacity and determination to formulate proposals to individuals who require reliable sources for the products being promoted. Moreover, there is an opportunity to provide some insights regarding the strategies for becoming a prosperous affiliate marketer on a platform with a substantial number of aspiring individuals.

Two goals done simultaneously. The advertiser will promote both the product and the program in which they are featured. It is possible that someone could be inclined to participate.

Time passes quickly. Despite having missed lunch, she is highly content with the tasks completed. Sleep time... .

Okay, it is highly unlikely that this will be completed within a single day. Nevertheless, this presents an insight into the activities undertaken by a dedicated member marketer throughout their advertising day. Is it truly foreseeable that this achievement is forthcoming at a distant location?

First Blog Post

Now is the perfect occasion for you to craft your very first blog post. You may be exceptionally energized or too anxious. However, your initial post is unlikely to be of optimal quality. However, do not allow that to impede you from maintaining communication with someone. I kindly request that you make your utmost effort and submit one. You will acquire knowledge and refine your skills through your blog and writing endeavors, yet do not anticipate achieving perfection right from the start. Becoming a proficient blogger, as it were, necessitates both financial investment and practical exercises.

It is important to bear in mind that as long as you possess above-average writing skills, meaning that you are capable of constructing a sentence and have some understanding of the subject matter, then you should be satisfactory. If you have conducted research on the internet, you may have discovered numerous methods to craft a blog entry. In this publication, we will develop a simulated validation framework that can be employed by individuals to craft exceptional articles. We shall employ the P.A.S strategy, renowned for its ease of implementation and its track record of remarkable success among numerous bloggers.

One of the remarkable aspects of this strategy is that it allows for the creation of a standard blog post devoid of any affiliate link. You may also leverage it for merchandise sales via your affiliate interface. In light of this observation, we will delve further into the intricate nature of the P: problem, An: unresolved S: untangle approach. We will also construct an exemplary provision

23

explaining the PAS policy to aid readers in gaining a better understanding of it.

P: Problem

As the aforementioned title suggests, it is indeed an issue. I require you to have a thorough understanding of your area of expertise and the audience it attracts. If your blog pertains to effectively reducing body fat while maintaining a healthy lifestyle, I kindly request that you commence the article by presenting the challenges to the readers. The most efficacious method to achieve this objective is by establishing relatability, evoking within the readers a sense that you comprehend their challenges and sufferings. Present it within the primary section of the article.

An: Agitate

In the subsequent section of the blog, it is necessary to promote the distress. You have effectively determined how to discern the underlying pain points of your readers. Currently, it is imperative to foster a stronger emotional connection with the readers. Evoke a sense of urgency in the readers, compelling them to promptly seek a resolution to their predicament, as they cannot sustain this current state. Furthermore, it is advisable to refrain from extensively addressing the matters, as doing so may project an image of helplessness and lack of cooperation.

S: Solve

Finally, you will now provide the readers with a solution to their problem. You will serve as their savior. This could potentially involve an associate being linked to an item that would enable them to resolve their query. It is indeed a response that you could present to your readers in order to gain their confidence. Endeavor to minimize the regular transmission of such communications to subordinate affiliations. It will give the impression that your main motivation is to derive financial benefit from them rather than bringing about meaningful change. Employ a methodology referred to as the 'poke, strike, impact, ensnare' to render three articles void of substantial content, and subsequently include an affiliate link within the fourth one.

In actuality or in reality, P.A.S (in real life).

You might have conducted online research on techniques to achieve a weight loss of 50 pounds. Within a span of four months, one can achieve the desired outcome by either consuming this magical supplement or adhering to a fitness regimen that costs $1,000. Allow me to offer you an opportunity to save valuable time and enlighten you with a certain revelation: none of these methods are effective. I have previously experienced the situation in which you currently find yourself, striving to improve your physical fitness, and have found it challenging to identify a viable solution.

I acknowledge that you have made numerous attempts without success. Notwithstanding all your efforts, you are unable to achieve the desired results. I am aware that it presents a significant challenge. You endeavor to ascertain a solution for success, yet find yourself encountering frustration.

In all sincerity, it is evident to both of us that living in such a manner is not sustainable. There are myriad of experiences that you have yet to encounter due to your obesity, which warrant considerable appreciation.

Based on my previous experience at that particular place, I can affirm this statement. I previously had a weight of 50 pounds. overweight. After diligently exploring all options, I managed to discover a viable solution amidst this tumultuous situation.

Through the implementation of the aforementioned regimen commonly referred to as "get fit," I successfully achieved a weight loss of 50 pounds. in only 4 months. I have not reflected upon the matter since that moment. I am finally capable of enjoying greater freedom and exploring a wider array of life experiences. If you are currently endeavoring to lose weight like myself, please click on the hyperlink provided below to access a webpage that offers a discount code for purchasing a duplicate. I eagerly anticipate witnessing you lead a healthy and fulfilling lifestyle, just as I am.

If you carefully review the aforementioned article, you will observe how I have adeptly employed all three techniques within the P.A.S framework. It is crucial to make it a primary objective to ensure a seamless flow throughout your essay. I would recommend composing your initial three articles without any affiliate links, providing free assistance to your new readers in order to establish trust.

If you opt to incorporate a member association, subsequent to providing them with complementary information, the likelihood of their conversion will be enhanced in comparison to withholding such communication. Moreover, do not unnecessarily fret over the process of articulating your essays in a myriad of perspectives. With the utilization of the P.A.S technique, one can swiftly elevate their blog's monthly earnings to $3,000.

Additionally, please ensure that you include an emphasized image in your blog post. You can avail high-definition images at no cost from numerous free websites, ensuring that the photographs are in HD quality and relevant to your blog post. Finally, if you approach this section in a systematic manner, you should encounter no difficulties in crafting an exceptional article for your blog platform.

Maintain a mindful awareness to refrain from the pursuit of perfection, as it ultimately breeds dissatisfaction. Instead, strive to exert your utmost effort and showcase it to the world. You will derive far greater benefits from grounded experiences than striving to peruse this book and achieve flawlessness. You are advised to employ this book as a manual and refrain from undertaking the task alone.

Nations That Reap The Advantages Of Affiliate Marketing Via Amazon

Several nations reap the advantages of Amazon's affiliate marketing program.

Amazon affiliate marketing is among the advantages extended to several nations. Nations such as Japan, India, and Canada have strategically positioned themselves to gain a competitive edge in the realm of international trade.

Nations such as Japan have effectively capitalized on the Amazon affiliate marketing program to establish it as their primary platform for international e-commerce. As a consequence, globalization has been accelerated within the nation and has fostered greater international trade in contrast to nations lacking a comparable infrastructure, such as Thailand.

Nations such as Canada are capitalizing on the opportunities presented by Amazon's affiliate marketing program, employing it as a means to stimulate their economy via electronic commerce.

In addition, India has capitalized on this opportunity by utilizing it as a global marketplace, leveraging its ability to provide services at a more economical rate compared to other counterparts.

Amazon Affiliate Marketing is a revenue-generating mechanism through which Amazon capitalizes on the sales of products listed on their platform. When consumers click on a designated affiliate hyperlink and proceed to make a purchase, the affiliate is remunerated with a commission corresponding to the transaction.

The countries that are experiencing the greatest advantages as a result of Amazon's affiliate marketing initiatives are those that possess dedicated Amazon websites and those that maintain a clientele in the United States.

In what ways can governmental policies contribute to the promotion of successful affiliate marketing?

A crucial initial stage in the implementation of affiliate marketing by companies entails gaining a comprehensive understanding of the regulatory framework established by the government.

In order to uphold compliance with applicable laws and regulations, it is imperative for individuals to possess comprehensive knowledge regarding the legal proceedings and requirements within their respective industry. The government has implemented measures to oversee and regulate sectors such as automobile, financial, and healthcare industries.

Ensuring adherence to these policies will significantly contribute to the success of affiliate marketing as a marketing strategy, facilitating the expansion of market share in regulated industries.

The article highlights the rise in popularity of affiliate marketing as a burgeoning platform for promoting and advertising various products and services. With the assistance of government policies, it has the potential to achieve even greater success.

There are a number of policies that can be implemented to address this issue, such as:

Financial incentives will be provided to individuals and entities who choose to make investments in affiliate marketing.

Amidst advancements in technology, we have implemented a streamlined online transaction system that entails significantly diminished fees and charges.

Setting forth a concise structure for the self-regulation of the industry.

One approach that governments can facilitate the prosperity of the affiliate marketing industry is by establishing unambiguous guidelines for industry regulation. They are also capable of fostering engagement in virtual platforms.

CHOOSING THE APPROPRIATE PRODUCT OR SERVICE FOR MARKETING PURPOSES

With the successful identification of your target audience and the niche in which you aspire to operate, the subsequent task entails locating the appropriate products and/or services to endorse to them. There exist various approaches to identifying products or services that can be offered to your intended audience.

Issues and Solutions

After identifying your target audience, you can proceed to ascertain their challenges and subsequently find remedies to aid them. In consideration of the specific market segment you have selected, compile a roster comprising a minimum of three issues for which you aim to provide solutions to the target demographic.

Here's an illustration:

Married professional mothers with children who are of school age and excel in maintaining a structured routine.

Issues encompass maintaining a familial schedule, orchestrating meals, and implementing organization.

Potential solutions include utilizing digital calendars, creating bespoke meal plans and shopping lists, and implementing organization strategies and tools.

After you have assembled a comprehensive inventory of issues and corresponding resolutions, proceed to explore reputable affiliate networks for the products that align well with your assessment.

A brief inquiry on ClickBank.com unveils numerous products that may be of interest for your promotion endeavors. Among these offerings is Get Organized Now, a widely recognized affiliate network that offers a diverse array of products across various industries for marketing purposes, including the option to promote your own products.

However, refrain from immediately initiating its promotion. Compose a roster comprising multiple entities. Then,

Perform some product research. Explore the origins of the creator and visually examine the masterpiece.

Take into account the product's rate of conversion, as well as the values and style of the creator.

Adhere to the desired brand voice that you intend to convey.

In the absence of personal referrals to validate their professionalism, I suggest conducting a firsthand assessment by acquiring their product and critically assessing both the product's caliber and the company's customer service. Ultimately, as an affiliate marketer, you are entrusting the responsibility of customer service to a designated individual or entity. It is imperative that you guarantee the provision of excellent customer care by them, as this is pivotal for maintaining the appreciation and trust of your audience towards the recommendations made by you.

Various Programs

There are numerous affiliate networks available that offer you the chance to reach out to your intended demographic and promote your offerings. Every network has its own idiosyncrasies and challenges that you need to familiarize yourself with as you become a part of it. Affiliate products are also available through exclusive programs that are not included in affiliate networks.

Several individual publishers, for instance, favor utilizing technology like aMember.com to establish their program. As a consequence, they will not be included in affiliate platforms. Merely conduct a search utilizing relevant keywords to ascertain the solutions that are most likely to yield the desired products.

In the aforementioned instance, we conducted a search on ClickBank specifically for Household Organization. Please initiate a web search on the Google search engine using the keywords "Household Organization" in order to discern the results. In our particular instance, the primary outcome yields a website by the name of Getorganizedgal.com, which offers solutions that are sought after and desired by the target demographic.

Nevertheless, no affiliate program appears to be evident; however, upon closer examination, it becomes apparent that she utilizes Teachable as the platform to disseminate her courses. Teachable incorporates an affiliate module within its framework. It would be advisable to consider reaching out to her via email to articulate your admiration for her merchandise (post-purchase) and convey the potential benefits your audience would derive from the establishment of an affiliate program for your platform.

Another online platform that emerges is Cozi.com, serving as a digital tool tailored towards family organization and management. The application includes a calendar feature, shopping and to-do lists, recipe management, meal planning capabilities, and a family journal component. If you satisfy the specified criteria, you are eligible to participate in Cozi's affiliate program, enabling you to generate income by endorsing their products.

Here are a few programs that warrant your consideration:" "Please explore these following programs:" "I would like to bring to your attention a few programs that you may find beneficial:

JVZoo.com

Affilorama.com

ClickBank.com

ShareASale.com

Associates at Amazon

eBay Affiliate Program

Affiliate of CJ

Market Thrive

Udemy.com

Skillshare.com

Each network possesses its own set of merits and demerits, and this is merely a subset of a larger array of considerations. Through the utilization of the Google search engine, one can access extensive compilations of affiliate networks, both general and those catering to specific niches. As an illustration, should you exclusively desire to vend organic commodities, you will be presented with an extensive array of choices.

Additionally, it is possible to conduct targeted product searches in order to identify suitable options for promotion. Subsequently, one can seek out the corresponding affiliate program links or establish communication with the relevant entities via email to obtain further details. While there are business owners who choose not to utilize affiliate networks, a significant majority actively engage with this approach, thereby providing a wide array of lucrative products for you to endorse. In the event that you are unable to locate one, it is always a viable option to reach out to the creator via email and express your willingness to provide assistance by showcasing your social credentials.

Profitability Analysis

Prior to selecting a product for promotion, it is imperative to ascertain its profitability. The profitability of the product can be assessed by reviewing the metrics displayed on an affiliate network. Should you find yourself collaborating directly with the product creator, it may be necessary for you to evaluate your assumptions subsequent to utilizing the product.

Please take into consideration the following points.

Generous Commissions - A commission rate of less than 50% for digital products is likely to yield minimal returns.

Elevated Selling Price - Should the commission fall below the threshold of 50%, the price at which the item is being sold is deemed high.

Are the profit margins substantial enough to warrant a price per sale that adequately compensates for your time and effort?

Conversion Rate - The majority of affiliate programs typically provide details concerning the conversion rate, encompassing the number of sales accomplished, or other relevant information to facilitate your decision-making process in evaluating the suitability of this option.

What is the visual presentation of the sales page? Although it may not be considered enjoyable information, it is an established fact that longer sales pages tend to yield better results than shorter ones for a significant number of target audiences. Has the sales page been meticulously designed and thought out? Is it converting?

Purchase it - Once you come across a product that you deem suitable for promoting to your audience, proceed with the acquisition of the item. If you possess sufficient influence or leverage, there is a possibility that you could acquire it without cost, or at the very least, obtain a complimentary copy for the purpose of assessment. Nevertheless, procuring it as a consumer is the most optimal approach to gaining insight into their operational methods and evaluating the suitability of the product for your intended consumer base.

Is there a rivalry? It would be advantageous to conduct a thorough search and identify alternative products that exhibit similar characteristics to the one you aspire to sell. If the product or service aligns with the current demands and preferences of your target market, the level of customer education required would be comparatively reduced.

Would you be able to generate additional search terms? - After ascertaining your decision to endorse a particular product, could you generate additional search terms in order to initiate the development of marketing materials?

What are your plans for promoting this product? - An additional inquiry that necessitates your consideration is the approach you intend to employ in order to promote the product. Are you intending to undertake a comprehensive campaign, or do you plan to integrate it through an embedded link within your blog's content? Would you be inclined to endorse it to individuals featured in your mailing list? Which section? The greater the level of precision with which you can strategize the timing, methods, and locations for the product promotion, the higher the probability of profitability.

Discovering a lucrative product can be accomplished with relative ease by selecting a well-suited niche characterized by a robust audience eagerly seeking the necessary solutions to enhance their lifestyles. It is incumbent upon you to ascertain your niche, ascertain the products that cater to your target audience's needs, and strategize on their optimal presentation.

Alternatively, you have the option to develop and produce your own unique, specialized products. Next, let us examine that.

An alternative approach to generate income as an affiliate marketer involves initiating the development of your own products and/or services to offer to your intended clientele. Collaborating with your target audience and acquiring customers through the promotion of your products and the publication of content could grant you valuable understanding of the audience that motivates you to develop a novel product exclusively tailored to their needs. The pricing of the product will vary based on its intended usage, with the possibility of being either complimentary or subject to a fee.

Providing Bonuses

One can incorporate their own products into the assortment by providing an incentive for acquiring another affiliated product. The supplementary product enables you to incorporate them into your repertoire, enhance your earnings, and potentially showcase further how you can address the audience's concerns.

Should the product creator grant permission, several affiliate systems provide the option to integrate your bonus product seamlessly into their sales funnel on the respective affiliate platforms, such as aMember.com or JVZoo.com. In alternative scenarios, it may be necessary to display resourcefulness and dispatch the bonus using an alternative approach. Nevertheless, a plethora of technological advancements exists that can perform this task on your behalf effortlessly.

Making Your List

As an affiliate marketer, it is possible for you to develop personalized products with the primary objective of cultivating your subscriber base. An excellent illustration could be a comprehensive list of guidelines aiding your audience in the process of choosing the optimal affiliate marketing software or establishing their inaugural webinar. Constructing a comprehensive list entails providing your audience with items that are both easily achievable and align with their genuine needs and desires.

Another Source of Income

Moreover, in the capacity of a product creator, you possess the ability to generate products that serve as an additional source of income alongside your affiliate earnings. It is possible that you could develop a more efficient calendar for organizing cleaning tasks, in comparison to the one you have been endorsing. Perchance you have crafted a comprehensive instructional program focused on maintaining optimal household organization, which you intend to market. After the creation of the product, one may engage the services of affiliates to act as sales agents.

As an individual engaged in product development, it is imperative that you ensure the acquisition of appropriate software, such as aMember.com, in order to establish an efficient shopping cart and potentially a membership platform. This will facilitate the widespread dissemination of your digital products and services to your specific target demographic. Furthermore, it is possible for you to utilize any of the aforementioned affiliate networks to feature your products and entice potential affiliates, thereby augmenting your revenue.

How Can One Cultivate Trust With Their Clientele?

How can one establish a sense of trustworthiness with their clientele? Now that you have obtained a comprehensive understanding of the strategies you can employ to craft a compelling blog with significant market potential, it is imperative to acquire knowledge on how to effectively convert your audience into paying patrons. This will ultimately enable you to transform your blog into a lucrative revenue stream. When executed with precision, one can swiftly surpass the goal of earning $100 per day and ascend towards achieving $250 per day and beyond!

There exist multiple methodologies through which a blog can be monetized, extending beyond the three prominently discussed strategies as outlined in

Chapter 2. The subsequent techniques outlined in this chapter pertain to the transition of bloggers from earning minuscule sums per month to generating a substantial income from their blog. Numerous strategies are available for utilization, and one is not obligated to employ every single one in order to generate revenue from their blog. With that being stated, you have the option to utilize all of them if you wish to do so.

Direct Sales

A multitude of individuals are engaged in the realm of direct sales. It is also renowned for its high concentration of individuals with substantial wealth, attributable to the flourishing industry. If one desires to optimize their earnings, engaging in direct sales could potentially prove to be the most effective approach. Although direct sales pose no significant challenges, they do demand a steadfast commitment. In contrast to the multilevel marketing (MLM) systems, there is no obligation for you to establish a downline or arrange your genealogy tree in a specific manner in order to optimize your earnings. Alternatively, you generate revenue from all the sales conducted via your distribution channels, in addition to earning a percentage from each individual who joins your downline. This renders it an exceedingly uncomplicated procedure, while also being uncomplicated and effortless to uphold.

Direct sales operate in a comparable manner to that of affiliate marketing. It is still imperative to employ a disclaimer, ensuring transparency with your audience regarding your financial gains from endorsing the recommended products or services. Subsequently, you may proceed with composing a discourse on those topics. Given that you engage in recurrent utilization of the same merchandise or services through direct sales, it is imperative to ensure that you consistently produce written content pertaining to them. An excellent approach to accomplish this is to thoroughly analyze various perspectives on the product or service's impact on one's own life and its potential benefits for others. As an illustration, consider the scenario in which you are marketing culinary items on behalf of a company engaged in direct sales. One may engage in conversations regarding numerous recipes involving these products and tools, encompassing both traditional and readily accessible options that attract initial attention, as well as unique and unconventional choices that offer delightful flavors. In this manner, in the event that an individual were to conduct a search query for a commonplace term such as "meatloaf," your page would be discoverable. Nevertheless, within the "related" section, they would encounter a multitude of uncomplicated recipes created with the specific products supplied by your organization, which deviate from their usual search preferences. This phenomenon engenders a compelling and captivating allure, prompting them to navigate further within your website. As a result, this augments your renown, amplifies the prospects of your content being shared, and enhances the prospects of generating revenue, should they elect to make a purchase from your company via your platform.

An additional advantage of direct sales lies in the potential to establish a structured framework wherein, upon enrolling individuals under your guidance, you provide coaching to enable them to generate a substantial income. One possible rephrasing in a formal tone could be: "This could encompass a straightforward measure such as establishing a Facebook group exclusively catered to your subordinate consultants, where they can participate in regular coaching sessions led by you, alongside receiving supplementary materials such as complimentary printables, informative handouts, comprehensive guides, comprehensive checklists, or any other resources vital to sustaining their progress." Given that you derive profits from the earnings they generate, this enhances your overall profitability. In addition, you enhance your potential to expand your audience by leveraging their platform to exhibit your blog as a source of inspiration for their customers. This, subsequently, presents you with the opportunity to generate revenue by promoting and marketing other products to them via alternative affiliate links.

When engaging in direct sales as a means to optimize the profitability of your blog, it is important to diligently heed the regulations and details outlined in the agreement. Not all companies exhibit complete flexibility towards bloggers. Bloggers often encounter a set of challenges when endeavoring to promote direct sales companies. One such obstacle pertains to the regulations that prohibit them from addressing any other products specific to their industry on the same platform where they are promoting the direct sales products. One additional policy observed in certain direct sales companies involves restricting bloggers from discussing the company once their blog surpasses a specific threshold of monthly readership, as it is perceived as unfair to other distributors. Such regulations may impede your capacity to promote these products or any others, hence it is crucial that you take heed. Please exert maximum effort in identifying a solution that possesses the qualities of adaptability, superior quality, and is deemed deserving of dissemination to others. Furthermore, refrain from sharing anything for which you lack passion or a genuine intention to actively engage with. If the recipients of your message were to experiment with the products and find that they fall considerably short of your purported claims, it is highly likely that they will perceive you to be disingenuous. Maintaining a commitment to honesty and transparency is vital in cultivating and preserving the loyalty of readers, thereby enhancing the likelihood of their patronage.

Funnels

Developing sales funnels is an effective method to generate revenue through your blog. Sales funnels are uncomplicated, yet they possess a significant influence on effectively converting your target audience from mere readers to loyal customers, provided that they are constructed in an appropriate manner. ClickFunnels is a highly commendable service due to its comprehensive approach, where they meticulously elucidate the entire process, guiding users through each step of the way. Moreover, they alleviate the burden of arduous tasks by diligently performing them on your behalf, leaving you with the simple and effortless task of seamlessly incorporating your funnel.

Funnels serve as a mechanism designed to guide a reader towards the initial purchase of a smaller product, subsequently leading them towards a larger product, ultimately culminating in the acquisition of your most substantial and most compelling offer. As an illustration, should you be engaging in self-help blogging, you might initiate your sales funnel by presenting an affordably priced eBook offer amounting to $10 or less. Subsequently, you would present your readers another compelling proposition: a downloadable course with a value of $150, attainable at a price below $50. Subsequently, you would proceed to proposing a consultation call or a one-hour coaching session, valued at $99. Following that, you will proceed to present to your esteemed client a tailored service solution that aligns with their specific requirements, founded on the insights garnered during the aforementioned conversation.

Undoubtedly, this particular funnel does not precisely adhere to the standard appearance expected of all funnels. If you do not possess coaching expertise, exclusively deal in products rather than services, or engage in any other similar business model, then it is necessary for you to modify this sales funnel in accordance with the specific offerings you provide. Additionally, it is not obligatory for you to remain within the price range of $10, $50, and $99. Alternatively, you are free to set the price according to your preference. The concept pertaining to pricing involves commencing with a modest fee, ensuring that it is affordable enough to eliminate any hesitation in availing the product or service. According to research findings, consumer decision-making is typically less deliberative for purchases below $50. Frequently, they will proceed with the acquisition. This initial proposition substantiates the caliber of your work and assists your prospective clientele in discerning the substantial value that you bring, as well as the magnitude of benefits you can offer them.

The subsequent proposal they receive should exhibit a higher price point, yet not reach the level of costliness as your ultimate offer. This proposition ought to be characterized by an equivalent level of excellence, profitability, and desirability. Additionally, it should be promptly extended following their initial purchase, ensuring that it takes place within a favorable timeframe during which you remain vivid in their memory and the educational material provided continues to captivate and hold value for them.

The second proposal will give rise to the third offer, which is significantly more substantial and should serve as an introduction to your ultimate offer. In the event that your offerings solely consist of products, this particular proposition may indeed constitute your ultimate and conclusive offer. If you are providing services, it is at this juncture that customers should transition from purchasing products to procuring your time in order to engage in a conversation with you. Subsequently, this would provide you with the chance to present an official proposal in person, thereby guiding them into the subsequent phase of the procedure.

Funnel processes may either entail substantial time investment and demand high levels of engagement, or they can be completely automated, necessitating zero effort on your part. By producing pre-recorded, enduring products known as "evergreen products," one can effectively automate the entirety of the process without the need for any modifications. These products, intended to retain their value over time, would independently perform all necessary tasks, eliminating the necessity for any manual intervention. In this scenario, your funnel would serve as a highly lucrative stream of passive revenue.

Enrollment and Regular Fees

Subscriptions present an excellent opportunity to monetize your blog. Numerous individuals who possess a skill or expertise beyond writing frequently express a penchant for establishing membership or subscription services in order to generate a steady revenue stream. These offerings are commendable due to the fact that through a membership or subscription service, one is necessitated to create only a singular entity that effectively caters to the entire paid clientele. As an illustration, consider the instance wherein you operate as a culinary enthusiast and content creator within the realm of gastronomy. Individuals who are part of your esteemed circle or have registered as members can remit a monthly remuneration to avail themselves of the privilege of accessing your exclusive culinary creations, premium discounts offered by your affiliated corporate entities, and comparable exclusive propositions. If you happen to be a coach who writes a blog focused on self-improvement, this premium subscription grants access to an array of benefits, including a monthly weekend course for members to complete and a live training call held exclusively within a private Facebook group limited to paying subscribers.

Not all varieties of blog formats are compatible with membership or subscription models; however, there exist numerous distinct styles that can be contemplated if you desire to integrate such features into your blog. Although these endeavors require additional time and effort to cultivate and sustain, they have the potential to generate a substantial income for you. If you possess an inclination towards pursuing such an endeavor, you must take into account the necessity of providing a service or product that aligns with the preferences of your target audience, to be offered on a recurring basis in accordance with the duration of your membership or subscription terms. Furthermore, you must demonstrate a steadfast commitment to consistently deliver the aforementioned product or service as per the pledged terms, without fail, on a monthly basis. Nevertheless, should you be inclined to make a dedicated commitment to this endeavor, it is not uncommon for numerous bloggers to earn substantial monthly incomes in the range of several thousand dollars through the utilization of these services. Additionally, it is not imperative to possess a substantial audience in order to commence your journey. You merely require the dedication of one or two individuals who are willing to subscribe, and from that point onward, your following will gradually expand.

Educational Programs, Merchandise, and Offered Solutions

Naturally, leveraging your blog's specific niche to offer and monetize courses, products, or services presents a commendable means of augmenting your blog's financial gains. While the production process of these items may require a significant amount of time, they can yield palpable results that can be presented to your audience as a means of generating income. This is a method that numerous bloggers employ to significantly augment their earnings by leveraging their platform. When executed properly, it does not necessarily have to be arduous or excessively time-consuming.

Courses tend to require the least amount of time compared to other options for monetizing your blog. If you possess a dedicated studio or a serene office space where disturbances are minimal, it is feasible to record yourself on video as you impart valuable knowledge, which could subsequently be transformed into an instructional video course. If you incorporate additional downloadable PDF files that provide written materials and interactive instructional resources, a comprehensive educational program is obtained. The pricing of these programs varies between $15 and $1000, contingent upon factors such as duration, content intricacy, and market demand. You can readily establish a collection of courses and monetize them by offering them on your blog for a specified charge. Subsequently, you can effectively promote these courses in conjunction with marketing your blog, and for every individual who enrolls, you will receive compensation.

Individuals create educational programs for a variety of purposes. Currently in the realm of blogging, there exist a plethora of courses covering a wide range of subjects, ranging from culinary skills to the art of instructing felines to traverse using a leash. Individuals exhibit a profound curiosity in widening their knowledge across a diverse range of subjects, which presents advantageous prospects for you. This presents you with the chance to conceptualize and produce goods or services that cater specifically to your target audience, thereby enabling you to generate additional, residual revenue.

The level of demand associated with the provision of products varies. For products of a straightforward nature, such as instantly accessible downloads and digital content, they may involve a relatively lower investment of time. For artisanal goods, the process of crafting them often spans a considerable duration. One could also contemplate the implementation of drop shipping, an alternative method that is relatively less prevalent in the blogging sphere yet can indeed yield additional revenue without necessitating any direct involvement with the product itself. In general, one of the most convenient approaches to offering products, if you are not inclined to engage in production yourself, is via direct sales and affiliate marketing.

When engaging in product sales, additional costs may be incurred due to expenses related to shipping, production time, and overhead expenditures. Nevertheless, a considerable number of individuals derive great satisfaction from acquiring items recommended by their preferred influencers. Hence, renowned bloggers like Ree Drummond, also known as the Pioneer Woman, have established and curated their own range of products. By cultivating a dedicated audience and providing them with products that align with their desires, one can effortlessly augment their earnings through the implementation of this approach.

Engaging in services is an alternative that demands a significant amount of time, yet offers the advantage of direct monetary compensation for your efforts. The prevalent services provided encompass various forms of coaching, consulting, counseling, or akin services. Nevertheless, you have the option to provide services pertaining to writing, graphic design, editing, virtual assistance, and related fields. The range of services you can offer is contingent upon your ability to deliver them effectively to your clients.

One of the notable advantages of utilizing services is the absence of the necessity to generate a product before engaging in sales efforts. Regarding the production of artisanal goods, one must not only invest considerable time and effort in the crafting process, but also exercise patience until they are sold in order to generate a financial gain. This implies that a substantial amount of effort is exerted without any assurance of recouping the investment of time and resources. When considering services, all it takes is crafting a compelling proposition and effectively promoting it. One does not commence any task until the compensation for the rendered service has been received. This implies that one should refrain from allocating excessive time and effort towards endeavors that lack assured outcomes.

Online Social Networks

Whilst social media communities in and of themselves may not generate revenue, they do enhance the potential to transform your audience into profitable clientele. In the presence of a social media collective, such as a Facebook group, the conditions are ideal for fostering a closer bond with individuals within the community. Contrary to the followers of your profiles and pages, individuals who are part of a group experience a stronger sense of connectivity to you due to the inherent nature of a group. Moreover, it imparts a feeling of exclusivity and intimacy with oneself. Establishing a collective with the purpose of hosting a community and actively participating within that community offers you the chance to foster stronger connections with your most devoted supporters and followers. This implies that by establishing a more customized interaction with them, you can foster a deeper sense of allegiance, ultimately leading to an increased level of loyalty. As you undertake this action, their level of interest in acquiring your products, services, direct sales propositions, and any other offerings at your disposal becomes heightened. Therefore, although your community alone may not generate any revenue, the relationships you establish within that community greatly enhance the probability of individuals purchasing your offerings.

Should you decide to pursue this course of action, it is imperative that you allocate your time to fostering a community in a sincere manner. Should individuals become members of your group solely to discover that its sole purpose is incessant marketing, it is highly probable that they will not remain in the group for long. Instead, dedicate your time to providing additional value and content within the group. Subsequently, at regular intervals, you may disseminate a promotional publication. In this manner, individuals have the opportunity to acquaint themselves with your persona and develop a favorable opinion of you by means of the collective. Consequently, when you present a product or service for their consideration, their receptiveness increases as they perceive your genuine concern for their well-being and recognize the inherent value in what you are offering.

Strategies For Monetizing Affiliate Marketing

"Remuneration based on ad clicks:

These search engines generate listings and evaluate them according to the bid amount specified by the website owner for every click originating from that particular search engine. Marketers engage in competitive bidding to secure a more favorable position in the ranking for a particular keyword or phrase.

The website that secures the highest bid for a specific keyword or phrase will subsequently be ranked as the top result in the PPC Search Engines. Subsequently, the second and third highest bidders, along with other bidders who have participated in the auction for the same keyword or phrase, will be ranked accordingly. Upon agreeing to a specific cost per click, your advertisements will be prominently featured on the search results pages.

What are the methods through which one can generate revenue in their affiliate marketing business by leveraging PPC advertising? The majority of affiliate programs solely compensate you when a purchase is completed or a lead is generated subsequent to a visitor clicking through your website. Your income may vary as it is contingent upon the content of your website and the fluctuations of the market for website traffic.

One should consider integrating PPC into their affiliate marketing program due to the comparatively simpler means of generating earnings as opposed to other non-PPC affiliate programs. In this manner, you will be able to generate profits derived from the click rates that your visitors generate on the advertiser's website. In contrast to certain schemes, remuneration is not based on the number of sales or actions undertaken.

PPC has the potential to significantly enhance the resourcefulness of your website. By integrating PPC Search Engines into your affiliate program, you can derive financial gain from the visitors who display no interest in your products or services. Those individuals who depart from your website and fail to return.

Not only will you receive commissions from individuals who actively search the internet for desired products and services, but you will also enhance your website's reputation as a valuable and reliable source. It is probable that those visitors who have successfully obtained the information or products they were seeking from your website will revisit your site in order to thoroughly evaluate the offerings you provide. Subsequently, they will ultimately return to peruse the internet for alternative merchandise.

This type of affiliate program also presents a convenient opportunity to generate supplementary revenue. As an illustration, in the event that a visitor navigating through your website utilizes the PPC Search Engine to conduct a search and subsequently selects the listings that have been bid on by advertisers, the advertisers' account balance will be effectively reduced as a result of this particular click. In accordance with this provision, you shall receive remuneration ranging from 30% to 80% of the bid amount tendered by the advertisers.

Pay-per-click advertising is not solely a means of attaining effortless financial gains; it also serves as a valuable tool for promoting one's own website. The majority of the programs provide the opportunity to immediately allocate the received commissions towards advertising expenditures with them, without any prerequisite of minimum earnings. This approach represents a highly effective method for converting general website visitors into a more specific audience consisting of potential customers who are inclined to make purchases of your products and services.

What are the potential outcomes of integrating PPC into your affiliate program? PPC typically offers readily available affiliate tools that can be seamlessly incorporated into your website. The prevailing tools include search boxes, banners, text links, and a few 404-error pages. The majority of search engines employ customized strategies and are capable of offering a white-label affiliate program to you. By implementing just a few lines of code, you can effectively integrate a co-branded search engine hosted on a remote server into your website.

The key benefits? In addition to increased revenue, there is also supplementary income generated. In addition, you will receive lifetime commissions after successfully referring webmaster acquaintances to the engine. Think about it. Where can one avail of these advantages while concurrently generating revenue for one's website? Gaining knowledge about the practical tools at your disposal for optimizing your affiliate program is a valuable asset and should not be disregarded. They serve as a means of generating additional income.

It is imperative to familiarize oneself with the operational aspects of integrating PPC search engines into the affiliate program, as failure to do so may result in the potential loss of substantial profit margins. The verbiage used in your content prompts the PPC contextual ad systems to display advertisements that are tailored to correspond with said verbiage. Native advertisements do not possess contextual relevance. On the contrary, they employ imagery that appears as miniature representations of the articles. When individuals interact with the native advertisement, you receive monetary compensation.

Remuneration based on the number of sales achieved:

When an individual interacts with your Pay-Per-Sale (PPS) option, whether it is integrated with textual content or visuals, their purchase is necessary in order for you to receive a commission.

Cost Per Action (CPA)

Pay-per-action offers remunerate individuals when their shared link is clicked, facilitating the access to certain form-based contents. You will receive monetary compensation when individuals complete the form. CPA presents a reduced level of impedance to the user." "CPA offers a more streamlined experience for the user." "CPA minimizes user obstacles and complexities." "CPA presents a diminished level of user inconvenience. Frequently, individuals merely need to provide their email address, enabling you to generate revenue ranging from $0.20 to one dollar. Not too bad.

Affiliate Programs for the Sale of Goods

Merchandise affiliate programs pertain to affiliate programs specifically engaged in the sale of tangible products. If individuals encounter advertisements on your website, you will not receive remuneration. When individuals engage with the advertisements by clicking on them. Compensation is solely based on the commission received for the purchases made by your visitors.

Strategies for Choosing Affiliate Programs

Numerous accounts of alarming experiences are recounted concerning affiliate programs and networks. People have been exposed to these messages on numerous occasions, to the point where some individuals are apprehensive about becoming part of such a group. The narratives they might be familiar with pertain to illicit initiatives or pyramid schemes. Essentially, this particular market lacks genuine, valuable products.

It is in your best interest to disassociate yourself from these fraudulent endeavors. It is evidently clear that you desire to align yourself with a program that provides excellent quality products, which you will readily support and promote. The increasing participation and significant achievements of numerous individuals serve as sufficient evidence of the existence of dependable and high-quality affiliate programs in existence. Consider the following elements when selecting one affiliate program over another.

Is the offer directly or indirectly linked to your specific industry or area of expertise?

Direct your attention towards the offerings of a program, rather than solely focusing on the program itself. Numerous programs are available to accommodate a diverse range of specialized interests. It is imperative that you carefully review their offerings to determine if there is a suitable match for your specific niche.

Has the offer been extensively advertised?

Conduct a search using the name of the offer or the name of the company and refrain from engaging with oversaturated offers.

What level of simplicity does the conversion point of the offer entail?

Ideally, you should seek out an opportunity that necessitates only a single click in order to receive payment. If such an occurrence is not transpiring, consider seeking opportunities that provide monetary compensation for each email or zip code that is submitted via a form. If such an option is not accessible, then consider examining opportunities that provide remuneration based on a significantly high percentage of sales.

What degree of adaptability does the program possess with regards to advertising?

Is it necessary to utilize the program's proprietary materials? Alternatively, do they approve of you independently creating your own materials? Can you use incentives? You would not wish to accumulate an excessive number of commissions, only to face the risk of being disqualified without receiving rightful compensation.

Do they provide landing pages that can be easily tailored to specific needs and requirements?

Does the program facilitate the creation of custom landing pages or does it offer pre-designed ones? Should there be any individual instances in their possession, can it be determined how numerous these variations are? Ensure clarity regarding the methodology employed by the sponsor in converting your traffic.

Is the usage of tracking URLs permissible?

To the greatest extent feasible, you aim to ensure the inclusion of each and every click derived from your online assets. Despite procuring traffic from platforms such as Facebook, it remains crucial to monitor and record your own clicks. In this manner, you will be able to discern the efficacy of different webpages and identify the most advantageous channels of paid traffic that warrant reinvestment.

Is the usage of redirect domains permitted?

It is advisable to ensure that affiliate programs remain unaware of the sources from which you acquire traffic. They possess the ability to effortlessly redirect their attention to the source of your traffic, thereby usurping it effortlessly.

Additionally, it is undesirable for end users to be presented with an excessively lengthy hyperlink when they hover their cursor over it. This is unattractive. Make sure you're allowed to use redirect links to clean up (and hide) long affiliate URLs.

What is the compensation rate for the program?

The appropriate method of analyzing this subject matter is undoubtedly by means of making comparisons. When conducting a comparative analysis of various offer payouts, it is imperative to possess a comprehensive understanding of whether an offer is logical or reasonable. As an illustration, suppose there exists an opportunity that you anticipate will generate high conversion rates, despite the relatively modest compensation. In comparison, a program with generous pay might appear more attractive, but its offer is associated with a significantly lower conversion rate.

What is the quantity of offers available within the program?

The greater the program's specialization in your specific field, the higher the priority you should assign to it. I am not suggesting that you refrain from considering offers from other programs; however, given that this specific program exhibits a specialization in your niche, it would be advisable for you to allocate a greater portion of your time towards promoting this program.

Is it possible to utilize a diverse array of conversion systems in order to promote the program?

If one possesses the ability to leverage direct, mailing list, content, and various alternative traffic conversion methodologies, it may be prudent to consider opting for such a program. Please ensure that you give careful consideration to everything stated above. If one comes across a highly adaptable program, it is possible to generate a higher income compared to a more inflexible system. Could you please explain the concept of a conversion system? A conversion system can be regarded as a mechanism employed to optimize the monetization of website traffic.

Affiliate Marketing encompasses a wide range of diverse manifestations. It is possible for it to be considered as a blog. It has the potential to function as a distribution list. It may manifest as an advertisement placed on platforms such as Google AdWords or Facebook. It could potentially be an article for which you have remunerated a blogger to publish. It could potentially manifest as an image featuring a promotional code, for which remuneration has been provided to an Instagram influencer for their posting. Irrespective of its manifestation, a conversion system can be regarded as nothing more than a utilitarian instrument. The focal point is centered around attracting traffic and effectively converting it into monetary profits.

Utilizing Camtasia for Enhanced Affiliate Earnings

Given the increasing number of individuals embracing affiliate marketing, it comes as no surprise that the level of competition in the field is intensifying. The task at hand is to surpass other affiliates and devise strategies to achieve the objective. Extensive guidance and instruction are also provided to these affiliates on optimizing their planning and program execution, aiming for enhanced effectiveness and increased earnings.

What more effective method exists to impress and engage potential clients and customers than by creating and distributing high-quality, dynamic screen recordings that feature seamless streaming capabilities. There is no comparable sensation to experiencing the fruits of your labor as your customers eagerly and enthusiastically await the opportunity to purchase your product in the immediate moment. This showcases the practical application of Camtasia. It has been substantiated that providing tangible offerings to customers can have an instantaneous and profound impact on augmenting online sales figures.

Acquiring trainings and education is not a prerequisite for comprehending the functionality of this system in relation to your affiliate program. Individuals of all backgrounds possess the ability to produce visually impressive videos, ranging from multimedia instructional content to informative presentations easily accessible on the internet. The process entails having customers positioned in close proximity and observing your desktop, as you present them with the necessary information through visual and auditory means. All of this was accomplished gradually and methodically.

For individuals who are not yet aware, could you please elaborate on the functionality of Camtasia?

With just one click, your desktop activity can be effortlessly recorded. There is no necessity to undertake the task of saving and compiling all of your files, as they are automatically recorded instantaneously.

It is easily feasible to transform your videos into web pages. After conversion, your customers will be able to access that specific page. Videos are more easily comprehensible and assimilated compared to the challenging task of reading texts.

Upload your pages. Disseminate them via blog platforms, RSS syndication, and podcasts. You may desire for your Camtasia videos to circulate and extend their impact to potential future customers. There is no better means of promoting oneself and effectively conveying a message than by ensuring widespread visibility across various platforms and webpages.

There are alternative measures you can undertake with your affiliate program utilizing Camtasia. You have the capability to generate exceptional multimedia presentations that have demonstrated efficacy in driving sales growth, owing to their ability to fully engage the senses. Additionally, this has the propensity to alleviate doubt among customers who are difficult to please. Minimize instances of refunds and customer grievances by implementing visual demonstrations that illustrate the proper usage and handling of your product. Complaints will be effectively mitigated since all pertinent information and the accompanying demonstration will be readily accessible to customers.

Utilize visual presentations to endorse and market affiliate products and services. This approach effectively redirects your audience directly to your affiliate website upon completion of the video. Maximize the effectiveness of the presentation by strategically including your site location towards the conclusion, offering attendees the opportunity to conveniently visit the site for additional information.

Significantly amplify your online auction bids by presenting your readers with a compelling understanding of the value you have to offer. According to the reports, auctions featuring images lead to a fourfold increase in the bidding rate. Consider the potential increase in height if videos were taken into account. Produce and distribute informative products of high value that can be marketed at a substantially elevated cost. The expenditure will be justified due to the utilization of the visually appealing, fully colored graphics menu and templates at your disposal.

Reduce the occurrence of miscommunication with your customers.

Efficiently demonstrating the desired outcomes right away enables a clear comprehension of the fundamental nature of your affiliate program. One advantage of multimedia is that the occurrence of mishaps is considerably minimized. It is there already. Outlined above are only a few examples of the valuable actions you can undertake utilizing Camtasia, profoundly benefiting your selected affiliate initiative.

Please be advised that the primary objective of utilizing Camtasia is to enhance the revenue derived from your affiliate program. While it may serve as a source of entertainment and pleasure, which does not truly justify the effort undertaken. Concentrate on the objective you have established and endeavor to accomplish it by utilizing the resources available to maximize your income.

Beneficial Technological Solutions for Affiliate Marketers.

After one has made the decision to pursue a career as an affiliate marketer, there are a plethora of tools and technologies available which serve to facilitate and streamline one's responsibilities. The current technological landscape encompasses an array of tools, such as website development platforms, email marketing and automation software, market research solutions, along with various others.

• Website Tools

In order to construct an exceptionally effective website, it is imperative to deliberate upon the appropriate selection of domain name, hosting service, website creation platform, and landing page automation system, to maximize productivity while minimizing effort and concern. The subsequent tools will assist you in completing all tasks.

• Domain Name

One of the primary steps to initiate your affiliate marketing endeavors effectively is to acquire a domain name, enabling you to create a website that effectively attracts your target audience. Select a designation that encompasses a key phrase, possesses brevity and simplicity for easy recollection, and employs a domain extension. Namecheap.com proves to be an exceptional choice for acquiring the domain at a cost-effective rate.

• Website Hosting

The subsequent necessity subsequent to the acquisition of your domain name is website hosting. It is advisable to consult the host prior to acquiring your domain, as there are instances wherein they provide a package where the domain is included at no cost when you make an upfront payment for hosting.

A respectable website is characterized by its high degree of uptime, exemplary customer service, and user-friendly interface. An advisable choice, especially for those who are inexperienced and uncertain of their abilities, is

MomWebs.com. Their customer service and administration is exceptional.

• Website Builder

You are also required to construct or have a well-designed affiliate website established. This is an exemplary and highly engaged choice, as it pertains to the utilization of self-hosted WordPress. You may explore the topic more extensively on the official website of WordPress at WordPress.org. (Please be advised that this is distinct from WordPress.com, as the latter operates on a self-hosted WordPress platform.)

This manufacturer is easy to use and cost-effective, or even available for free. Importantly, it seamlessly integrates with search engines, which continue to highly value WordPress.

• Landing Page Builder

After completing all tasks, you will be in need of a greeting page generator. Currently, you can accomplish this task free of charge by utilizing self-hosted WordPress, simply by creating a new page. However, it will not possess a comparable level of automation. Automation can prove to be a valuable asset in augmenting your income, as it relieves the burden of manual labor. A decent decision for mechanized greeting page software is Instapage.com. If you happen to use a robust platform such as Infusionsoft.com for your marketing efforts, it is already integrated within the system. This specific software will automate the flow of information in your pipelines in a manner that will create an illusion of turning your website into an Automated Teller Machine within a short duration.

• Email Marketing

Email marketing is an essential aspect that cannot be overlooked. It is considered one of the most effective and significant forms of marketing present in contemporary business practices. Indeed, even social media marketing can't match the force of email marketing. This suggests that you will need to both capture leads and transmit emails in an automated manner.

AWeber.com is recognized as one of the most prominent choices in contemporary times, accompanied by the notable appreciation received by ConvertKit.com and ActiveCampaign.com. In addition to your landing page builder, these tools will automate to a significant extent.

• Market Research

As an affiliate marketer, conducting extensive market research is imperative to ensure the maximization of your efforts and to prevent them from being in vain. Failure to conduct proper research will result in engaging in futile actions that yield no outcomes. Refrain from making unwarranted assumptions and instead engage in meticulous research. One may conduct research on their competitors by utilizing software such as iSpionage.com, while trending topics can be explored by employing tools like Google Trends.

- Traffic Generation

Purchasing equipment aimed at enhancing traffic generation can be a significant means of establishing a prosperous affiliate marketing enterprise. Ultimately, a substantial influx of specifically targeted individuals is imperative to achieve the desired outcomes you envisioned when establishing your objectives and aspirations.

AdEspresso.com by Hootsuite is a highly beneficial tool for those who intend to execute numerous social media advertisements, as it simplifies the process significantly. You will have the capability to display aesthetically appealing and fully optimized advertisements across various leading social media platforms.

23. Facebook Ads - Employing the Facebook pixel on your website enables you to execute retargeting and remarketing initiatives directly through the Facebook platform. Subsequently,

you initiate an advertisement exclusively targeted at prior visitors, a strategy that has proven effective in augmenting both website traffic and sales figures.

24. RecurPost.com - Upon activation, this application autonomously disseminates your blog posts to the social media platforms of your choice, in a randomized manner. Additionally, please remember to dispatch an email notification. When you publish a fresh blog post, kindly notify your email subscribers through the automated blog post sharing functionalities provided by your email marketing software.

• Tracking and Converting

The additional tools intended to facilitate your journey towards becoming a lucrative affiliate marketer encompass instruments aimed at monitoring the efficacy of your efforts and transforming your audience. Every website must implement the utilization of Google Analytics. It is offered at no cost and operates exceptionally well.

Taking everything into account, Google remains the foremost search engine. That suggests a strong inclination on your part to adhere to their recommendations. For the purpose of monitoring interfaces, a suitable choice would be PrettyLinks.com.

You have the ability to configure your website in a manner where, upon detection of explicit terminology, the software will automatically insert an affiliate link into that particular term. That is an exceptional approach to automate your recommendations and effectively monitor clicks and conversions.

• Content Marketing

To enhance the traffic for your target interest group, it is imperative to create and distribute content that caters specifically to their interests. In order to generate persuasive content, one must conduct thorough research, ensure its clarity, and make it enticing. Moreover, it is imperative to ensure that you consistently publish content on a trustworthy and frequent basis. These devices have the capability to aid you in attaining that objective.

25. Conducting research often leads individuals to resort to the conventional and widely-used resources of Google Search and Google Website Tools. That is the place where you should commence. However, there are excellent paid software options available that can be utilized to a much greater extent, depending on the specific subject matter you are investigating. Some recommended approaches to consider include conducting searches on social media platforms, exploring information on competitors, and analyzing their internal data through the purchase of their products.

26. Revision – Prior to publication, it is imperative to ensure the readability of any content intended for dissemination, including blog posts or articles. To successfully accomplish this, it is imperative to thoroughly understand the target audience and familiarize oneself with the terminology they commonly employ. Subsequently, it is advisable to attain fluency in the language or, if necessary, engage the assistance of a proficient individual.

Additionally, one may avail of tools such as Grammarly.com to facilitate the editing process. In any event, that is the primary focal point. If you lack a clear understanding of what is correct, the software has the potential to perplex you.

27. Visual Assets - Eventually, it will be advantageous to generate visual

assets for the purpose of enhancing blog entries, social media updates, the production of eBooks, and other related content. An ideal solution for individuals without graphic design expertise would be to consider utilizing Canva.com. However, it should also be recognized that engaging the services of a skilled graphic designer holds undeniable value in this context.

28. Planning and Coordination - There are numerous tasks involved in marketing and scheduling, including strategizing the promotion of your affiliate business. Fortunately, CoSchedule.com provides a comprehensive marketing suite that includes a marketing calendar, content organizer, social media planner, and more. Alternatively, you may consider employing an individual to assist you in devising

and generating content for your affiliate business.

There is no necessity for you to undertake every task independently. You have the option to engage the services of a proficient content writer, as well as utilize private label rights content to augment your existing substance. Incorporating advantageous marketing-focused technologies is imperative to thrive as an affiliate marketer.

It is imperative to thoroughly review the terms and conditions of any technological product or service that one intends to acquire or utilize. This is essential as certain provisions may explicitly forbid engagement in activities involving affiliate marketing. It is advisable to familiarize oneself with the rules, as doing so will provide a comprehensive understanding of the proper utilization of each purchased device.

Creating A Viral Product

Equipped with affiliate links and your unique selling proposition, promote your entry into the field. How else should a victorious person like yourself announce their arrival? With a bang! Here's my go-to strategy for every important product launch I promote.

A viral product is a high-quality digital product with advanced distribution capabilities. This digital product promotes my affiliate URL. It could be an ebook or report with my affiliate link. It could be a program where my affiliate link appears in the client interface.

Now, the catch is, I distribute the viral product for free. Yes, for FREE. Why would I give something away for free if it's highly valued? What outcomes do I expect? Assume you receive something lucrative, free of charge. Wouldn't you feel unique? Wouldn't you feel fortunate? Wouldn't you feel ecstatic? Shouldn't you share that feeling with your closest friends? You relatives? The people you converse with on your favorite online forum?

That's why it's called a "viral" product; it spreads rapidly, at an exponential rate. Imagine each person recommending my viral product to 5 friends. 1 prospect can quickly become 5 prospects. Multiplying the number of prospects by 5 yields 25. 25 prospects can quickly become 125 prospects. Et cetera. It can quickly become an unstoppable cycle in the first few days. Many people experience this regularly, often for months or even years. Still, I'm generating clicks from an ebook I published 3 years ago!

Creating a viral product is easy. What are your strengths? If you know programming, program. Write ebooks and unique reports if you can write. Create a downloadable video or audio product if you have a talent for videos or television. Hire a consultant from websites such as www.elance.com, www.freelancer.com, or www.odesk.com if you are unable to do any of these. Ensure proper packaging and transport of the finished item to your location.

Voila!

Promote the viral product on your landing page for visitors to download. Ensure rules are followed.

Ensure to explicitly notify your guests about the free download of the mentioned product. Most people hesitate to download anything online, assuming there are no freebies in reality or on the internet.

Ensure to CLEARLY inform downloaders that they can share the software. Occasionally, that reminder helps significantly.

Using a viral product is a crucial component of the effective marketing technique called viral advertising. Virtual world viral advertising is essentially verbal promoting. You need individuals to discuss the product you are elevating to produce that abundantly required buildup.

Key elements of viral marketing to focus on are:

Viral marketing leverages existing networks. No need to create a network of connections.

The business message should be easy to spread. It must be evident from the earliest stage. An elaborate message would render the viral advertising battle meaningless. If you want your business message, such as promoting your website's link, to be effective, make it appear quickly and conveniently.

The message must commonly course in the business. The goal is to reach as many people as possible. The way to achieve that goal is to promote a consistent business message. Entrepreneurs should promote flow with minimal obstacles. The message should replicate independently. These should be kept in mind while creating a viral marketing strategy.

Your suggestion must be of quality. Allow us to demonstrate this adage via a commonly used method. Imagine your company provides a package of products. How can you popularly advertise it? You can use the suggested methods to provide a free trial of your product for a specific duration. This suggestion is of quality. Exposing more people to your product will lead to them recognizing its worth and sharing it with others. After their trial ends, they must ask for the complete version. Here is your unexpected suggestion. Assess the advantage of replacing your initial investment based on recent information. ROI is achieved when everything else is your net benefit, as individuals will consistently profit from your product due to the exponential nature of viral marketing.

You need an unexpected proposal. Give your bread and spread due attention. The goal of viral advertising is to provide your products and services. Your unexpected suggestion is your products and services. Now convince them to purchase your unexpected suggestion after grabbing the attention of potential customers with your quality recommendation.

Members should receive profits. The most effective weapon in viral advertising campaigns is the consistent use of the word "free." Providing complimentary items or services to potential customers is a long-standing practice in advertising, both offline and online. It effectively utilizes innate human tendencies: the clever principle. Treat others as you wish to be treated. Beneficiaries of your giveaways will feel obliged to reciprocate your generosity.

Following these principles of an effective viral marketing campaign will ensure a successful outcome for your website. Jimmy D is a valuable asset for viral advertising. Tan's Viral Ebook Brainstorm. Jimmy's extraordinary creation will become timeless viral advertising. To master this effective marketing, try Jimmy's book.

Key Factors for Setting Up Your WP Site

1. Do not install WP on 'yourdomain.com/blog,' instead install it on the root domain. Ignoring this is not the optimal approach.

So, watch before installing. Delete the installation and reinstall WordPress if you do it.

2. If you can afford SSL certification, choose it as it improves search engine rankings. Refer to your hosting's FAQ section for SSL setup instructions. Hostgator's shared hosting includes shared SSL.

3. Use a CDN as soon as you set up your site on WP. This single action saves bandwidth and enhances loading speed. Utilize this guide to learn how to set it up for your site. Read the guide below to speed up your WP site before setting up a CloudFlare account.

4. Choose primary and secondary colors for your website: Primary color sets the base and is used in the logo, navbar, footer, popups, etc., while secondary color is used for links, buttons, and other small decorations. A website with haphazardly used colors appears chaotic.

Test various colors by writing a dummy article after installing the site theme. Primary and secondary colors must contrast each other. Finalize your site's color scheme with Adobe Kuler.

5 favorite blogs with their primary color HEX codes:

Buzzfeed.com - #e32

No alternative way to express the given statement in the same number of words.

"Mashable.com - #00ae

neilpatel.com - #f16334

"Hongkiat.com - #26519e

5. Avoid duplicating your competitors' website appearance. People remember

only visual things in a busy world. It's a missed chance to stand out if your website resembles your competitors.

Many niche sites neglect this, which gives us an advantage to present ourselves better. Refer to the color scheme or design of any unrelated authority site for inspiration.

I shamelessly used the color scheme from a top SEO/Blogging site for my own site. I named it the 'Parasite Color' technique, where you take advantage of existing design elements from a unrelated established website.

6. Limit your website's fonts to just two, like the colors. One font for content and another font for headings, Nav Font, Logo, Sidebar, etc. Use readable Sans-serif fonts that are not too thin or loud, suitable for both desktop and mobile screens in this modern age.

Here's a list of contemporary Sans Serif fonts.

Lato

Open Sans

Montserrat

Use Source Sans Pro.

Railway

You can use serif fonts like Quando or Sanchez to be creative and complement your sans-serif font.

7. Check the appearance of your site on mobile and tablets while editing it on the desktop.

I neglected one aspect, resulting in rendering issues and an unpleasant appearance on mobile for my old site. Utilize Google's Mobile Friendly Tool to assess your website's mobile user friendliness and implement suggested changes.

8. This last tip about site setup is my highly opinion.

Don't ask for excessive suggestions from others. Confusion will intensify. Continue pursuing actions based on well-informed decisions for your website.

Don't ask for suggestions on themes, color advice, font suggestions, and so on. Thoroughly research before deciding, then stay committed.

Don't refrain from seeking suggestions. Don't linger too much in the loop of suggestions and counseling, even if they come from experienced individuals. You will be more perplexed.

Prior to proceeding to the next topic, Content Writing. I'll demonstrate the method to optimize your WP site for maximum speed.

Ashwin Singh advised me to use this trick for achieving faster website speed on WordPress.

Here are the specific steps:

Add W3 Total Cache Plugin to Your WordPress Blog

Visit: W3 Total Cache > Browser Cache.

Activate feature below.

Set expiry header.

Assign eTag

Enable gzip compression for HTTP.

Get Js & Css Script Optimizer Plugin

Enable the (WP Settings > Script Optimizer) plugin after installation.

Disabling Jetpack is recommended as it causes incompatibility with this plugin.

Ensure plugin options below are enabled.

Use Dean Edward's JavaScript Packer for script compression.

Merge all scripts into header and footer files.

Use CSS plugin.

Merge CSS scripts into one file.

Caution: This plugin may impair some of your JavaScript functionality. Ensure proper site check after plugin installation.

Important step. Use it if functions won't work.

Use CloudFlare

Ensure enabled options in your Cloudflare account.

1. Navigate to the "SPEED" tab and select the option to minimize JS, CSS, and HTML.

2. Navigate to the 'SPEED' tab, scroll and activate Rocket Loader. Select 'Automatic' under Rocket Loader. (Most Important)

Newly added sites on Cloudflare may take time to show the effect due to changes in Name Servers (NS).

Optimize your images and server to achieve a 90 GTmetrix score.

Follow the steps above for a 50% completion of building an Authority Amazon Niche Site that generates $1000 per month.

Also, 50% involves content writing, promotion, and backlink building.

In summary, here are the key points we have discussed thus far:

Choose a niche related to your personal experience with products in that category.

Create keywords by adding modifiers to the main word relevant to your niche and sub-niches during keyword research.

Understanding your niche is crucial for knowledge research. Study extensively the niche's history, preferred brands, popular products, additional features for an extra cost, and the like to enable authoritative writing in articles.

Avoid copying your competitors' themes and designs when setting up your domain, hosting, and site.

Don't compromise on the design of your website to make it stand out. For the initial 2 months, maintain a minimalist sidebar and avoid incorporating advertisements or banners onto the website.

Now, let's get to the exciting part - Content Writing and Representation.

Utilize Analytics and Tracking.

Don't expect to earn money simply by placing affiliate marketing links on your site. Maintain constant monitoring of your actions and the performance of the links. Every affiliate network should provide a reporting section to track link performance.

Check these reports frequently for emerging trends. All the links at the top of your articles consistently outperform the ones at the bottom.

Rearrange the products to increase conversion rate. If certain links consistently do not perform, remove them to improve conversion rate and avoid drawing attention from advertisers. If you're noticing poor performance of multiple links, try switching them and trying new ones.

It requires time to grasp what works and what doesn't, but once you do, you'll have a few articles that consistently perform well and become your profitable assets.

You should check both the affiliate networks' analytics for link tracking and set up Google Analytics for your entire website.

Get audience demographics and analytics for improved product selection. If your audience is mainly in Europe and you only promote products shipping to the United States and not Europe, your conversion rate will be low.

Engage readers prior to selling.

Build relationships with your readers through collecting emails, engaging on social media, and providing helpful assistance so they come to you when ready to make a purchase. Respond promptly to engage with readers by replying to comments and questions.

It may be time-consuming but it enhances the relationship with the reader. Enhances their sense of connection, demonstrates care and value for their opinion. All trust-building actions lead to loyal readers who return to purchase your products.

Social media. Social media. Social media. Join if not already. Social media platforms can be both painful and delightful, but they are your best friends to grow your followers. Additionally, they provide a fantastic means of connecting with your readers. Not having Facebook, Twitter, and Pinterest hurts your website's potential. Identify the most effective platforms for your niche and use them frequently.

Discover your readers' preferred sites and social media platforms to establish a connection. Discover the audience's location to promote your website and featured products where they congregate. Pinterest can be a surprisingly effective traffic-driving tool, sometimes more than Facebook and

Twitter. It's particularly useful for affiliate marketing.

Design a vertical pin (735px by 1102px) showcasing one of the featured products. Your pin can showcase the product or a creative element related to the post, linking to the website page featuring the product. Alternatively, you can directly hyperlink to the affiliate link and lead them directly to the advertiser.

You can use social media management websites like Hootsuite, where you can plan out what to post, when to post and on which social media platform to post it on. Observe your social media engagement and analytics to gain insight on your audience.

Knowing your audience improves affiliate marketing success. This will prevent overwhelm from social media. Remember your original supporters who helped build your traffic. Some of your early subscribers or followers may become your best customers in the future. Maintain a relationship with early followers as your traffic grows.

Linking boosts Google rankings

Internal linking is when you link to a webpage within a website rather than the homepage.

Google recognizes advertisements as advertisements. Google recognizes deep affiliate links as part of the page content. Deep linking enables links to appear as part of the content being linked to, bypassing them as advertising. Deep links are named so because they direct you beyond the homepage.

Deep linking allows Google to index these links, improving link juice. Google may display your page when someone searches for the product. Affiliate marketing articles have deep links, so Google ranks them higher.

Linking decreases bounce rate, increases page views and subscribers. Deep links are advantageous for readers as they lead directly to the desired page.

You want to increase your page's authority, and deep linking can accomplish that. Hidden, non-indexed pages benefit from deep linking. Adding affiliate marketing to your website is highly beneficial for monetization, visibility, and traffic due to the deep linking nature of most affiliate marketing links.

Create content with SEO in consideration.

Embedding affiliate links in an article is excellent. If Google can't find your articles and your traffic doesn't grow organically, people won't see it. After writing an article, it is published online. Nothing else needs to be done.

If you write with SEO optimization in mind, you won't need to later tweak the article for Google to find it. Writing high-quality content promptly catches Google's attention.

Conduct SEO keywords research to identify article content. For advertiser and product searches, use the same keywords via the affiliate network. This will enhance product compatibility, increasing site credibility.

Building The Perfect Website

Develop a website that completely caters to your chosen niche and target audience after identifying them. Fortunately, you can create a great website on WordPress.com without any coding skills, and it's been empowering people to bring their ideas to life for over ten years, all for free.

WordPress is widely used, with over 25 million websites currently utilizing its platform. Many renowned companies like Samsung, Ford, and Pepsi rely on this popular website platform. It is free and user-friendly, but for a more professional look, consider upgrading.

Those with minimal technical knowledge but an interest in affiliate marketing will find it easy to add content to the already created site. Once the site is established, anyone familiar with basic word processing software can easily add new content with a few clicks. Each new post is designed for easy discoverability by Google's search engine. The site you create will have an equally appealing appearance in both traditional and mobile formats.

There are numerous WordPress templates available, both free and paid, which means you can still create a unique website despite the abundance of existing WordPress sites. With some thinking and work, you can find a suitable one to attract your desired customers. You can also create something completely unique if you feel like it. In addition, WordPress provides numerous plugins for additional site functionality.

Select an appropriate domain that reflects your niche and appeals to your target audience. A memorable URL is crucial when starting afresh, so choose a name that facilitates this.

Hosting companies like HostGator.com or GoDaddy.com allow you to search for website URLs matching your site's name. You should aim for maximum brevity while ensuring that the URL is easily distinguishable when spoken. Always choose a URL with a .com address as this is what consumers are going to assume your website is regardless and going with a .net because the .com version often just means you will be marketing for someone else's website.

Theme

Select a theme for your website, as it will greatly impact its overall appearance. Moreover, installing a theme after building the majority of your site may potentially undo some of your efforts due to its impact on the site's functionality.

Install and activate a new theme for your WordPress website. Access this area by clicking on Appearance in the left sidebar, then choosing Themes. There are galleries with various free themes, but you also have a limited selection from the start. You have the option to install a free one, a paid one, and/or any downloaded from elsewhere.

You can upload a downloaded theme or template from your backend admin page. Results of WordPress themes can be found by searching in the directory. You will find your theme options and search for them based on name or visual appeal. You can go to Add new theme to install additional themes.

Think about the content you will present

To sell effectively on your website, remember you'll need more content to support your goal. To ensure proper organization, it is crucial to comprehend the content you'll create amidst its variety.

Fortunately, a simple website with fewer options avoids confusion for users. For user-friendly navigation, it is advisable to separate the contact page, submission form, and FAQ. Make sure your website has the following at least:

• Homepage: The page where your URL leads users; includes essential details about your site and highlights its unique aspects compared to similar sites.

• About Us: Present a relatable version of yourself to readers. Balancing a created persona with genuine life details is crucial for a unique and repeatable blog.

Ensure your website is mobile-friendly for all devices. Related concerns about mobile websites are discussed in a later chapter.

Remember these layout tips.

Consumers typically judge a website within three seconds, making a good first impression crucial for affiliate marketing success. To ensure a good user experience, make sure the homepage is easy to navigate and understandable.

Moreover, you should provide them with a clear navigation guide that highlights the different sections of your site and its offerings to prevent confusion. Use clear call to action buttons. Minimize ambiguity for new site visitors to increase their likelihood of staying.

The era of the highly crowded website is gone, always remember. Focus on the rule that less is more these days. For a personalized touch, opt for a sleek and minimalistic style with subtle accents that reflect your personality. Currently, utilize white space wisely so that all elements on your page are deliberately and meaningfully positioned.

This design philosophy helps your website load faster. If the loading screen takes up all three seconds of the viewer's attention, there will be lots of page views but no engagement. Make your site load in approximately one second by trying all possible methods.

SEO Considerations

Without updating your website's SEO, a well-designed, fast site featuring high-quality blog posts won't help you succeed. SEO is essential for attracting visitors to your website through general search engine searches. All search engines, irrespective of your preference, utilize automated programs to gather and store information from numerous webpages across the internet. These details are summoned for every search you make.

SEO acts as a signpost for automated programs to perform their tasks more efficiently. Improved site navigation boosts search rankings. Keywords were popular because they helped web crawlers classify website content. Regrettably, the system wasn't sustainable in the long run due to the ease with which people could manipulate it by adding irrelevant keywords.

Key phrases

Web crawlers have shifted towards prioritizing key phrases to enhance the system, as they offer the same function while making it harder to manipulate and ensuring the relevance of websites in search results. To optimize search rankings, tag every page, blog post, and item with relevant key phrases. You can modify site key phrases through metatags in the navigation menu, while each new post will include a tab for meta data.

Begin with your niche and target audience to determine the best phrases for your site. Choose words that are precise but not overly specific, to avoid general search results but still ensure your website appears in the search results. Simply enter the phrases you are considering and see the results to make sure you're on the right track. Maintain a balanced level of competition to ensure the possibility of being successful.

For an affiliate promoting all-natural dog food, the core concept words cannot be relied upon. Instead, emphasis should be placed on the all-natural aspect, by beginning with details about the food. Shorter key phrases receive more weight from search engines than longer key phrases.

Repetition is key: Once you have decided on the key phrases that are right for your site, it is important to ensure that they show up everywhere that they are relevant. The more times a key phrase is properly used on your site, the higher chance of appearing on the front page of search results in that category. Be cautious with their use, as if your site lacks effectiveness for a specific topic, users may stop clicking on any of your links.

Prioritize having a defined strategy: Avoid recklessly deploying your key phrases without an established objective. Maximize your search ranking by knowing your phrases, their usage, and purpose. Find consistent keywords and phrases to improve search engine rankings. Success may not be achieved with this approach for all keywords, but focusing on specific search aspects will eventually yield desired results.